Delphi Series
Vol IX

Susanna Lang
Jennifer Grant
Christina Lovin

Published by Blue Lyra Press

ISBN-: 978-1-7338909-6-0

Blue Lyra Review, a journal of diverse voices, is a division of *Blue Lyra Press*, and it is currently closed to new submissions.

Blue Lyra Press publishes several times a year and accepts poetry and flash fiction chapbook submissions under 25 pages during two months throughout each year: January and July only. Send directly to the email below.

Writings or images published on the *Blue Lyra Review* website or in print are copyrighted by the creators. Explicit permission must be obtained from the copyright holder for use of any such material. E-mail bluelyrareview@gmail.com to obtain contact information for those writers and artists.

Blue Lyra Review & *Blue Lyra Press* are independent and rely solely on the generosity of donations so **please** support the arts: (www.bluelyrareview.com/donations/).

SUBMISSIONS: direct to email with bio, acknowledgments, and table of contents

FACEBOOK: www.facebook.com/BlueLyraPress

TWITTER: twitter.com/MESilverman_BLP

PURCHASE: bluelyrapress.com/

CORRESPONDENCE: bluelyrareview@gmail.com

Front Cover: Dorothy Englander's "Outside" (2019)

Note to Readers

It is just the second decade of the Twenty-first Century and we are facing uncertain times. We need stability: Stability of the economy, Stability from the government, Stability with our health, and Stability in our lives—and yes, that is with a capital "S". With so many things shutting down and/or changing, I am deeply saddened to say that *Blue Lyra Press* will be joining them. I am distraught by this. However, I can definitely say it has been a fun experience both reading all these wonderful writers and working with so many great individuals.

These last three poets, like the writers in *BLP* before them, are truly dazzling. Lang, as Angela Narciso Torres states, is "a piercing light." The way she makes these two dozen women artists come alive is like being in the breathing space between the viewer and a great painting. Lang writes in "Terra Incognita": "we make things, as if we'd suddenly remembered / their flickering images projected on the walls of a cave. / (But we never entered the cave.) / Some of these things we make / inhabit our bodies, / then learn how to breathe on their own." Truly, she brings these works and these women's artwork into breath.

Wonderfully balanced in the middle like the perfect sandwich is Grant's *Year of Convergence*. As Sue Walker states, Grant has an "unmistakable, singular poetic voice that takes measure of the human heart." Like many of her poems, she shows us something from the world around her only to draw a deeper meaning from it as she does in"What Doesn't Kill You". Grant writes: "Drive down any road here and you'll see it: / row upon row of green—pale in the spring / then darker as the seasons make their change / through summer's heat and storm, into the fall / when what was vibrant fades to golden hues. / Then stripped, staked, and crucified in the fields. / Slouching to leather, tanned soft as the skin / of chamois, hung to dry in the rafters / of black barns, their doors open like the mouths / of the cancerous dead and dying."

Finally, Lovin's poems are indeed "wry, elegant, {and} heartfelt", as Richie Hofmann states. Trust me, you will want to know and feel the work within *God of Sparrows.* Lovin shows us the reality of loss as she does in "Fledge" when she watches new fledgling birds die from a crow: "the breathless tumbling / through space as the watchful god of sparrows / and numbered hairs turns away. For one moment, / every bird must be there—hanging on a breath, / then gaining potential and height. But hope /is a feathered thing that drops into the pit /of my stomach, for I find nothing on the ground /below, too many long, sad stories down." It is this captivating breathlessness that draws the reader into her wonderful 'sad stories'.

Table of Contents

Self-Portraits

by

Susanna Lang

Table of Contents

Acknowledgments

I am grateful to the editors of the following publications, where these
poems first appeared:

Alexandria Quarterly: Gelatin Silver

Cobalt: On Rereading Helen

december magazine: Unnamed Road

Ekphrasis: Self-Portrait XII and *Physalis,* or Winter Cherry in the
spring/summer 2016 issue; Self-Portrait, 1620 in the fall 2016 issue

Escape into Life: Drawing; Self-Portrait as the Allegory of Painting;
Studio Visit

The Interpreter's House: Studio Visit: Later

Masque and Spectacle: Studio Visit: New Work; Woman with a Double
Bass; Everglades

Painters and Poets: Self-Portraits

Slippery Elm: Icarus

So to Speak: Terra Incognita; Cartas, 1986

south85: Self-Portrait at 80

Sugar House Review: Lost

Verse Daily: Lost (republished)

Terra Incognita

And I'm generating, I'm generating,
oh my babies by the millions where
will you all sleep?
—Helen Degen Cohen

It's like when one of the dragons who patrol the edges of the known
    world
breaches beside the ship we did not know
we were sailing, water spraying off its scales;

or when a long-forgotten word swims into our brain
and finds its exact spot in an ongoing sentence,
though we're not sure we ever learned it:

we make things, as if we'd suddenly remembered
their flickering images projected on the walls of a cave.
(But we never entered the cave.)

Some of these things we make
inhabit our bodies,
then learn how to breathe on their own.

Some glow in the dark, poisoning our blood;
or they open the door into rooms that were not here
before; they sing our mothers' songs, wring themselves out like a mop.

Like the brain stem, that deeply embedded—
the urge to put things together like red and blue Legos,
to make something not in the instructions that came with the box.

Self-Portrait XII
Young June Lew

They stand close together, these robes
that do not clothe bodies,

hems and yokes embroidered
with delicate vines. Only one

has turned toward us, the sleeves
cradling a violin, and over one shoulder

a vivid wing. No hands or bow,
yet a melody hovers in the dark

enclosure of the canvas. The artist
has come for the gallery opening

but is not at home in our language.
She wants to know, do we understand.

She has always felt a stranger, she tells us,
having come to this country

from a distant place. In this, she says,
she is like us all—aliens,

invisible one to the other. Perhaps music
will open our eyes, help us remember.

If not music, paint.

Self-Portrait at 80
Alice Neel

She has a brush in one hand, paint rag in the other.
Nothing else, not even clothes.

Yes, her breasts sag.
Her belly sits in her lap like a child.

But look at her right foot—
flexed, ready to go.

She leans forward, chin raised,
eyes on the canvas.

Even though everyone's gone.
Left her with this body in its chair,

this body at night in bed,
in the empty room.

The work heals and heals
until it can't.

More Desire
LEDANIA

In the beginning was color.

Lime and orange and turquoise sprayed straight from the can, and these
beaked and fishtailed creatures, antlered and ships-sailed, mouths open,
a cacophony outside our range of hearing. *I used to dance* plays the DJ
as Ledania climbs the scaffold, arms full of color and boots of music.

She sends us a birthday card on her own birthday, festival of painted
bricks; sings *cada día tengo mas ganas de pintar y pintar* as she blows out
her candles.

Birthday after birthday she will never grow old, never grow tired of these
delicious fumes, this power to make new things in all the cities where
houses threaten to slide roof over foundation down the precipitous
mountains.

When she is queen, she will proclaim an end to white walls, unpainted
viaducts, power-washed brick; and every baby will be born with a story in
her mouth, like a spoon.

Choreography
Nicole Livieratos

Join us, she calls in the city street
but it is not her voice calling.

Why are we still drinking from these empty glasses
she asks
but it is not her glass, or her hand on the glass;
not her mouth, not her throat parched for water.

Have we even looked for the key that opens these doors
she wants to know
but she is not the one who flings her body
against their unyielding locks.

Not the one dressed in red who turns himself
upside down and walks himself around like a pinwheel
till he is right side up again, but still not through.

She does not reach for one bleached shirt after another,
does not run full speed into any wall.

But she is the one who lined these bodies up like words
in a well-constructed sentence, set them in motion like
animated portraits;

and that might be me who cannot get comfortable
in the red plush chair, who will not turn the page
to write a new story.

Spectres
Eva Hesse

Half unseen
flickering
like balky wicks

or dancers,
yellow, not
yet dancing

> *In the Gare du Nord someone is playing the piano.*
> *No one can board the trains*
> *and still the notes fly loop de loops in the vaulted hall.*

Spectres like
dancers, arms
raised, knees bent

> *Sol Lewitt will send her a postcard, Magritte's man in a bowler hat*
> *walking away across the Seine. He will tell her to make nets*
> *with things in them, and she will. She will, for a while.*

—not sure if
nets, if arms
will catch their

loop or leap

Lost

Patti Smith

She learns that the things she carries—her camera,
the coat she wore to speak with the dead—recoil from her,

fall away. They do not come when she calls, and she calls.
Her bags still at the hotel, with the book she'd read

and reread, the photos taken in perfect light. All gone.
She's left to walk through the city streets

with only the clothes on her back, and the dreams
she never fails to record in her notebook.

   * * * * *

She took her camera back to the cemetery
but the season had changed, or it was still spring

but no longer evening, or the wind was blowing
from another quarter. The light was sharper

or more diffident. She found herself thinking
of coffee, its fragrance cupped in her hands,

instead of the voice she had come there to hear.
Too much to ask that it speak once more.

   * * * * *

I touch the keys in my pocket, again and again;
in another city, the plastic card to open the door.

The weight of my phone. Both gloves in my purse.
I keep the books that matter all in one room

with a door that closes, drawings and prints
on every wall, desk cluttered with intricate carvings.

But neither the dead nor my dreams will stay with me,
and there are friends I have not seen in years.

                    * * * * *

Our lost do not come back like the cats
that walk into the next room in order to cry out

and wait for us to call. It is tempting to think
that the lost return to the places we found them:

a favorite earring into the hands of the woman
who made it, the book with its marginal notes

to the dusty corner of a second-hand bookstore.
Perhaps I dreamt and then lost the words
on the page, the song I remember her playing.

Unnamed Road
Jungjin Lee

Not only the road wanders without a name.
This shrouded woman climbing the steps beside the road

and the man who, arms akimbo, walks through another frame
where a low wall marks the edge of the road.

And then a child, sitting alone, unprotected.
Perhaps an abandoned truck without a license.

But for most of its length, the road has been stripped
of everything but its own surface, shining a little

in the black-and-white light of what has happened and happened again,
in these unresolved angers and inexcusable lapses.

Here a doorway, outlined but unopened.
There an infinite expanse of bricks that do not adhere to each other.

The light is constant and unforgiving.
Unwilling to turn away.

Cartas, 1986
Elizabeth Catlett

She sits at the kitchen table
in her city hat, holds the day's
letters in her hand: *Still no rain.*

*No one remembers a winter
dry as this. We saw how that boy
was beaten and chased across*

*the highway up by you. His poor
mother. Be careful.* Each time
she left the house, that refrain—

Be careful. She hasn't been careful.
*We're thinking we'll plant sorghum
this year. Better than corn*

*if it doesn't rain. Over in Brownsville,
they've got more rain than they can handle.*
The soil will be dry, hard, not receptive

to seed. She remembers. They will wait now
to plant. And in the next months:
Even the sorghum is a loss, brittle and brown.

Too late for rain. She remembers, sky
the same ghost color as the fields.
Seems like everything goes down.

*We saw how the market crashed, almost
like when you were a girl.* She's never
been careful, but never lost

what she has, these lines and pools
of ink, this clean white page.

Woman with a Double Bass
Suzanne Valadon

The room is mostly dark, though an unseen window
halos the woman

and her bass, the woman's arm draped around the instrument
like a sister—

her hands, the bow, her impassive face, all bathed in light.
The woman's skirt

drawn in at the waist, belling out to the ankles, a fiddle shape—
the fabric dark

as the fingerboard beneath the woman's pale hand.
They are waiting

for the painter to finish. In a moment, they will begin to sing,
their deep voices

so closely harmonized, it will seem
they sing with one voice.

Studio Visit
Alicia Henry

She has raised congregations on her walls—
believers scissored out of paper, felt, burlap,
linen, their eyes and mouths stitched shut
or cut wide open to speak, cry, sing. She will not
speak for them, requires us to listen closely, study
these faces layered on faces like masks that hide
nothing. One couple is formally dressed in white,
no legs beneath the woman's gown, the man's left leg
abbreviated at the knee, the stump rounded.
A child's ivory shape at the woman's heart.
On another wall, the left-over legs, headless
bodies, heads resting beside bodies. They have all
come to say their piece: the room hums with their voices
like a church where the organ has just finished playing.

Self-Portraits
Käthe Kollwitz

She was old even when she was young.
Kept late-night vigil, the lamp
shining white on her smooth skin,
the unmarked page, her stilled hands.

The same eyes look out from
her sketch at 60, my age now.
The years between, all war years.
Her gaze disembodied, no paper

ready for her pencil, no hands,
only a smudge of charcoal
haloing her face. The same
downturned mouth.

She knew even before her child
was born, what emptiness
would hollow out her body
at his death; had swallowed

the grief of all the mothers who sat
by deathbeds, heads in their hands
and the long night folding
like a cloak around their shoulders.

Topography of War
Doris Salcedo

If there is a single chair, the wood stained dark, polished by the weight of our bodies and the weave of our clothes,

you can sit on that chair. You can rest.

If another chair is set across from the first at the same table, a friend can join you. Maybe there are glasses on that table, a bottle of raki.

But if a thousand, more than a thousand chairs are piled every which way, light and dark, slatted and spindle-backed, in a vacant lot in Istanbul where a building was torn down, its inhabitants scattered—

only ghosts will find seats on those chairs.

They are guests at the table we set for them, time and again, here and in Bogotá, in Bruxelles, in Marinka, Lahore, Calais. So many chairs. So many vacant lots.

Drawing, 1968
Gego (Gertrud Goldschmidt)

It is near the end of the story and long after
the war has ended (she would never discuss
those years, or say whether the keys to the door
had vanished silently into one of the many rivers
in Hamburg or if they cried out as they fell)
when the lines turn
back
    on them-
  selves, tangle
         and knot,
    opening up
            a space inside
       or beside
the route, and then
       without any obvious
intervention or resolution, find their way
forward again. Stop just short of the
edge.

Studio Visit
Virginia Griswold

The sculptor had to cast her own hand
in plaster, her hand with its just-acquired
ring, to know what it felt like to be married.
The vows were not enough: she had to feel
her plaster hand in her hand of flesh,
feel it made new by this small round,
all five fingers curled to hold the things
she now reaches for, Osage oranges
with their bumpy skins, unpalatable flesh;
arches on the underside of mushrooms
she'd gathered from the damp wooded paths.
These spheres and domes are not what
she used to mold. She has the photos: sharp
pointed things, broken things she made before.

Self-Portrait, 1620
Sofonisba Anguissola

She knew the nearness of her own death
by the lengthening of her nose in each successive

self-portrait, the draining of color from her cheeks
and hair. In this late work, her hands are emptied

of tools, spinet and books, unmarked by paint
or the splattering of glue she'd boiled

to prepare the canvas; one hand tucked
into her skirt, the other quiet on the arm

of a wooden chair. She still meets our eyes,
lips a thinner line than in earlier years

when she might not have been as young
as she made herself appear. She is not resigned—

not ready to go, despite the mourning drape
of her robe, the simplicity of her head dress

and impoverished cuffs. Her age gleams
against the flat dark behind her.

She meets her own gaze as easily as ours.

Drawing
Jim Ann Howard

She led me down a path to where water
surged over layers of sedimentary rock,
stories told in the grammar of earth

and water, ochers and graphites:
floods, upheavals, the long miracle
of creation. And she told her own stories,

the time she found a gray bat, recently dead,
brought it into the kitchen so she could draw
the outstretched wings, ribbed like umbrellas,

its knee crooked, claws extended, soft fur
at the nape. It's been years since we stood
together by the falls, the bat long dead. But here

it is again, in colored pencil and ink wash, as if
these wings could dance once more above the water.

Everglades
Jungjin Lee

Beneath the cypress, dark
sucks out all the air, and

    *

Glimmer of light on water.
The photographer's feet are wet
but she will not notice until
she has already turned back, after

    *

The egret will emerge later, caught between
that impenetrable black and the shining
water, wings widespread to carry
its slender neck, legs that dangle,
a brief fan

    *

White, no touch of darkness, no taint

    *

In its own world it is an ordinary
beauty. Nothing in this place
takes notice, except perhaps

    *

When a white bird rises from darkness,
even if it cannot know who else
might also see because
the photographer sees, is it
anything more than

Gelatin Silver

Nancy Marshall

Her river is a sweet black swamp
shadowed by trees and illuminated
by the rings formed when insects touch

the silvery water. A fallen branch,
its leaves not even a memory,
lies crossways to the current, dark

near the darkened banks, watery
in the sunlight. The birds hide,
silenced by the camera.

She can pause—on an island? bridge?
nothing as unstable as a boat—and frame
her shot. Nothing will move, nothing more

will be lost. The woman whose body
lies parallel to the fallen branch
will stay forever, knees floating

in the shallows, dark head
turned away, over a marble shoulder.

Icarus

Jyl Bonaguro

It was a failed crossing. Only his torso was found, ribs
and what lay above and below the bone: heart and the other

organs, muscles across the chest and groin. Just that much
of a man washed up on the beach. The skin heavy and white

as marble—a miracle that this body could fly at all. So many
have risked the currents, air or water. On another beach

a toddler, face down in the lace-edged tide, red shirt
and sneakers that someone knotted that morning. What if it were

my son, nails gritty with sand and hair slicked back by the sea?

* * * * *

A woman kneels, hammer in one hand, chisel in the other,
searching for the form buried within the marble: torso

of a young man, unmarred but inert. He fell; everyone knows
the story. He'd wanted everything, as every boy does.

The sculptor has felt that desire, has been tempted
as he was by the heat that stripped his arms of feathers,

but she has never had to wait, unknowing, the sky a bowl
that has been scrubbed too clean, while he launched himself

from his high wall, only to find a hard landing on this empty beach.

* * * * *

It was dawn. A light wind feathered his arms as he rose
into the welcoming air, never doubting that it would carry him

home, to the arms that waited to draw him close and then
release him into the rest of his life, that expanding vista.

Studio Visit: New Work
Ann Worthing

If you hold earth in your hands—
a clod of dirt from where you dug

in the garden—it will crumble
to dust. Light scatters

in the late afternoon, becomes
branches, leaves, a boy's

skinned knee. If you look at anything
long enough—this tree, these

four boys—it falls apart.
They are playing beneath

the wide-armed tree, feet
floating in air, their faces

blank: they could be anyone's
boys, they could be my boy

at that age, with his friends.
They could be light

refracted into color.
Memory does the work

of earthworms, breaks
the image down, so you see

the form that burns
within an angled ray of sun.

Self-Portrait as the Allegory of Painting
Artemisia Gentileschi

She turns away, brush just touching the canvas—
her first stroke. She paints herself absorbed
in the craft she knows herself to have mastered.
For this enactment of her great passion, her breasts
are covered, brown apron over the green of a dress
that shimmers as she moves, showing off her skill
with a palette. The good light of a well-placed window
gleams on her cheek and brow, her forearm,
the sleeve pushed up to the elbow like any worker.

Last night I dreamed that I went up a gravel road
toward a room where she waited, somewhere in the mountains,
among fields of sunflowers the color of Mary Magdalene's
penitent gown. In the dream we spoke, neither English
nor Italian. When I look in the mirror, she is there.

Studio Visit: Later
Alice Berry

What's left—bobbins, scraps
of fabric, reds and pumpkins
in one bin, blues in another.
A jacket, dark as its corner.

I remember tea in a fairy tale
harem splashed with glistening
silks that spilled from hangers
and shelves, from full-bodied

manikins. The light
now wintry, filtered through
high-set windows,
power switched off,

worktable bare. Ready.
For a year she did not enter
this studio, not sure what the room
was still good for. But out of a duffel

she pulls her new shawls, the fractured
lines like the quilts once sewn
by Dahomey women, whose squares
never lined up—they knew

that evil must walk a straight path,
can be foiled by angles and corners.

Physalis, or Winter Cherry

Mary Delany

She had lived long in the real world—the court,
   a loveless marriage and a loving one, both

husbands gone. Now 72 in an era when death
   came to most at half her age, she invented

a new world of cut paper and watercolor, in appearance
   precisely like the gardens of her old world, except

that it decayed more slowly and with more grace.
   In this "mosaick," the winter cherry gleams

against black ink, each pod a different stage, allegory
   of the ordered life: unripe and gold near the top

of the single stem, then ardent red, and at the bottom
   a paper fruit inside the actual fibers of a rotted husk

like the filigreed setting for a jewel, the cage imported
   from a real garden like the one she'd made,

first art, with the husband she loved. In her Eden,
   each bloom and seed distinct in its black bed,
   she would not build walls to keep death out.

On Rereading Helen

Here
are my edible skirts, says the earth, or is it the book?, here
are the colors you can live on. Here
is where you eat everything
alive.
—*"On Reading Tranströmer," Helen Degen Cohen*

You'd already feasted on the menu and its lists—galingal root,
lemon grass, coconut broth, steamed squid—before we arrived
at the Thai restaurant, but you still ordered soup & noodles. Here
are my edible skirts, you said in the earth's voice. Or was it the book?

You never liked poems written in the second person: they restated
what you already knew, who'd lived it, or they spoke past you
to some other you. But here, I want to tell you (not someone else),
in this market where I go alone, are colors you could have lived on,

winter squash speckled green and orange, carrots fanned out like
a peacock's tail, moon-white leeks, bronze and copper tubers,
frilled arugula, bushel baskets of apples with old names. Here
is where you would have eaten everything,

skins and all, the women carrying baskets, men with children
in their arms, molten honey and crystallized ginger, cheeses
and preserves set out to sample, rounds of bread. Everything
alive.

Notes

These poems grew out of conversations with women artists at the Hambidge Creative Residency Center. You need only look at the count published by VIDA: Women in Literary Arts to see that women are underrepresented in publications and reviews, and similar counts have been made for museums and galleries. I wanted to celebrate women's art, and to open a virtual gallery of works that especially move me. Beyond that celebration, I wanted to explore the ways in which our art, even when it is not literally a portrait of our bodies or a retelling of our lives, becomes the way in which we recreate ourselves. I am grateful to the women who are creating beauty every day, and especially to those who invited me into their shows and studios and conversations. Most of these artists and the works I reference can be easily found online, but I'm including notes for those who are more difficult to discover.

Helen Degen Cohen (1934-2015; Terra Incognita and On Rereading Helen) was born Halina (Halinka) Degenfisz in a small town near Warsaw. She survived the Holocaust in hiding. A painter, a writer of both fiction and poetry, and a teacher, she was a founding editor of *RHINO Poetry.* She was also a dear friend, who helped me reshape many of the poems I wrote during the last four years of her life. The poem I am responding to here was among those she brought to our writing circle for critique.

Young June Lew (Self-Portrait XII) is a Korean-born artist who now lives and works in San Francisco. She came to Chicago for the opening of her show, *Everyday Saints,* at the Andrew Bae Gallery, and I was able to speak with her there. Her new work includes faces for the first time, but in this poem I responded to an older painting, where invisible bodies inhabit the robes.

Nicole Livieratos (Choreography) is an artist whose work spans dance, choreography, performance and installation. She has done extensive work with arts integration in the schools and at the High Museum of Art.

She lives in the Atlanta area with her husband, the painter Alan Loehle. Both are old friends whose life in the arts has long been an inspiration for me.

About the Author

Susanna Lang's most recent full-length collection of poems, *Travel Notes from the River Styx,* was released in 2017 (Terrapin Books). Other collections include *Tracing the Lines* (Brick Road Poetry Press, 2013) and *Even Now* (The Backwaters Press, 2008). A two-time Hambidge fellow and a recipient of the Emerging Writers Fellowship from the Bethesda Writer's Center, her poems and translations from the French have appeared in such publications as *Prairie Schooner, Columbia Poetry Journal, Cider Press Review, The Literary Review, The Slowdown* and *Verse Daily,* as well as *Blue Lyra Review.* Her translations of poetry by Yves Bonnefoy include *Words in Stone* and *The Origin of Language.* She is currently translating the poetry of Nohad Salameh and Souad Labbize. More information available at www.susannalang.com.

Year of Convergence

by

Jennifer Grant

Everything that rises must converge
—*Flannery O'Connor, Pierre Teilhard de Chardin*

Table of Contents

Dedication

This collection is for my beloved and our son.
We three will always be a family.

Acknowledgements

Many of these pieces fell together in the weeks and months following Poet Mary Oliver's death and coincided with my son's move across the country to pursue his own creative dreams.

Blue Light Press poetry workshop participants and Poet Diane Frank were indispensable in sorting the poems out. Many of these are cento inspired pieces.

The title *Convergence* is a bow to all the poets, prose writers and lyricists who have paved the way for the rest of us. May we all continue to be healed by their words. And rise.

A Simple Sea Song for My Father
Published by Bacopa Literary Review, 2019

Poem of an Ordinary Girl
A Cento type poem using Grace Paley's Collected Stories as a diving off point.

While Reading Bishop
A Cento of sorts from pieces of poet Elizabeth Bishop.

Packing Away Childhood Books
Inspired by my early favorites: Louisa May Alcott's *Little Women, Little Men, Jack and Jill, Eight Cousins, Jo's Boys* and *Under the Lilacs;* Charlotte Bronte's *Jane Eyre;* Lewis Carroll's *Alice's Adventures in Wonderland;* Agatha Christie's *Murder at the Vicarage;* J.M. Barrie's *Peter Pan;* L. Frank Baum's *The Wonderful Wizard of Oz;* and T.S. Eliot's *Old Possum's Book of Practical Cats;* and an added book on Feng Shui...

My Father's Closest Friend Sings
Uses two lines from a 1960s Donovan Song.

Contemplating Convergence
A Cento using lines from Flannery O'Connor's work, Conrad Aiken and Johnny Mercer.

January Elegy for Mary

For the gatherers who come flying
I stand with un-feathered arms
flung barn door wide
toward an icy expectant sky.

I'm blue as a lapis jewel,
blue as a lonely goose who
no longer has a hatchling
to share nursery rhyming words.

The V swoops toward me,
two dozen whooping and cawing
a cappella creatures who croon
an eccentric, melancholy tune.

How effortless and focused they wave,
sway in unison. My own metronome
broken, tripping over sidewalk words
rather than releasing soaring birds.

With binoculars I squint, crane
my aching neck, funereal witness
to Mary Oliver's Winter ascent.

A Simple Sea Song for My Father

The song you heard singing in the leaf (seashell) when you were a child is singing still
—Mary Oliver

1
He says the sea is a gulf
of unfinished stories.

*Cast a spell, or your pole
and reel the Big One in.*

Daddy describes the unfurling
of tales as schools of fish.

Some arrive as polished
coins rosier than wine.

Others are jittery sequins
entangled in green,
goblins of sticky slime.

The job of the fable fisher entails
patience and a dram of luck.

I hold my breath and this red reeled
pole so tight my tiny hands tingle.

2
In dark rain I remain landlocked
in my study staring at a salt lamp,

the last remnant of an angling
trip shimmers in tangerine light.

I pick up the lightning whelk,
roll it around in my achy palm.

A few grains of sand drop
from its cold, dry mouth.

Lifting the shell to my ear
I hear an angler's siren song,
taste Florida brine on my tongue.

Time to follow my father's lead,
take his sacred reel to sea and troll.

Poem of an Ordinary Girl Reading Grace Paley's Collected Stories as her Piano is Hauled Away

Breathing out my shyness in jagged puffs,
the history between us heaves in and out.

I point to my heart where I've fastened
a shiny new zipper onto a devil red dress.

A few errant marks,
flaking white school chalk
remains on my hands to lather off
later, if I remember.

Perhaps we were purposely thrown
together into this familial sea,
garbage floating in a hazy litter
of love and leafy green vegetables.

Once I played you as virtuoso,
enticed through spring and summer
in and out of dogwood bloom
and then the looming laurel.

Both made me sneeze and you
gifted a secret fistful of tissues.

No more faith-filled grandparents flutter
from my memories. Those tweeting birds
are dead at the bottom of their pristine cage.

No noxious kitchens or fuming bedrooms
during my simple Wonder Bread childhood.

Until you and that damned metronome!

Still it ticks, ticks, ticks in my addled head.

Swaying, straying too close behind me
while I practiced and you taught me
more intricacies than scales.

I still do not forgive you.

While Reading Bishop the Week of her Birthday

Elizabeth Bishop (Feb. 8, 1911-Oct. 6, 1979)

1
The sky quivers in delight,
an invocation of sacrifice.

The narrow space of life
where wings of angels fall off—

In the last stages of decay,
her secrets dormant, underrated.

Like dining upon honey
and small shiny trigger fish,
she's now considered sophisticated.

What slow changes ensue
under wavering compass needles.

A space clear as grey
tempered glass.

Oh, my own sky is dead.

2
Feverish as an atom
I scarcely dare look

         up

               or

                    down.

No one knows what kind of bird
I am, big wings of poison folded

prayer-like on my featherless back.

Flying a little way at a time,
I embrace confused migration.

Too pretty in dreamlike mimicry
Is it homage? Or fear of flight?

3
Everything occurs in waves:
I'm burning in drowned green.

Acting as a skeletal lighthouse,
I endure browned mangrove islands.

Below me, slivers of gilt,
lobster pots and masts scattered
among wild jagged rocks, shells.

I want, wait and wish
not to be a monument
surrounded by a weak
white sky.

Packing Away Favorite Childhood Books on my Birthday

I wish for a wicked wind
to howl wildly and not whisper
its answer to my repetitive,
rewound question: *Now what?*

Once a plucky sort of girl,
nodding my stringy blond hair,
hiding from Mother crouched
behind her gold velvet chair.

You can't see her for she's out,
Mother said and I tittered,
imaginative and willful.

Never fretting over fancy
untold stories, I scribbled
words in erasable pink ink.

My recipe for sunshine
proved unsuccessful as the roof
of the family house finally flew off.

Everything—thoughts, feelings,
money, birds, butterflies
and illness blew away
with a cornucopia
of winking Black-Eyed Susans.

Their oddness won't cheer me,
perhaps a drop of scotch,
or more of an amber shot?

I can no longer wait, but must.

Just as Louisa May, the Brontes
and Agatha Christie—
I must.

My Father's Closest Friend Sings about my Nickname

The book of your life fell open
beneath a bright blue canopy
of sky, above splintered earth.

Nature's music pulsed slow,
a grassy octave not too high

or low.

Starry blossoms, pops of color—
fire red monkey-flower, pearl pink
lady slipper—caught my keen eye.

Your younger sister named aptly,
a sunny yellow gloriosa daisy,
lanky black-eyed Susan.

Your identity had to be a lesser tree.
Depressed and rigid shrubbery
with leaves hard and sharp.

Junipers form in large patches,
climb and arise to high altitudes,
sacred spaces, places like Tibet.

Baring berry-like cones in bright blue,
same hue as your ever blooming eyes.

Gaelic forebears of your dad burned
such twigs to cleanse, bless and protect.

Other family members used
the seeds to swill bathtub gin.

Jennifer, Juniper, hair of golden flax
Jennifer, Juniper, longs for what she lacks.

A Misty Morning

Somewhere in Florida, on a desolate interstate highway that pushes cars north and south and dumps them into a turnpike that flows east and west, a family of three drives a blue Honda at dawn. The sleepy sun wears fog as a shroud and she questions why a family of three is travelling with such dizzying speed on the Sabbath. Why indeed, asks a giddy group of purple pansies wiggling wildly roadside. Even an overgrown billboard mouse wearing a black-buttoned jumper and white gloves wonders why a family of three does not stop by to say hi or stay at the happiest place on this planet and instead barrels toward an airfield where only metal nosed aircrafts and angry passengers co-exist. A family of three bypasses worlds of wizards, whales, animated mice and ducks and abandons that blue Honda in short term parking lot row L. Then with heads slung low, shuffle off to the Delta ticket counter. It is here, at TSA pre-check, this family of three disintegrates. Like water droplets suspended near the Earth's surface, a shadow couple creeps foggily back to an empty car.

Mid May just before the Flower Moon Blooms

I'm sure it's a Whippoorwill chanting,
his throaty whistle echoing darkness.

Do you hear him?
It's 2 a.m.
and Beloved snores a response.

A nightjar beckons me outside
under the guise of a full moon.

Mama once told me darkness revealed truth,
probably a lie told to little ones who refuse
to rest their weary eyes.

The only fact that holds
is a devourer of galaxies
millions of light years away.

A vacuum that inhales
worlds in its path.
Not even light escapes its pull.

It's how my insides feel.

An astrophysicist said
to know these monsters exist
is "humbling."

How must I look,
swaddled in mint green sheets,
with cryptic blonde plumage
and mouth agape in mourning.

Black holes are born
when a colossal object,
a supersized star, collapses on itself—

A bottomless Florida sinkhole lurking
in the heart of another universe.

Little Whippoorwill,
are you out there?

Three tiny frogs pitch themselves
at the transom window of my bedroom.
Their familial shadows glued in place,
committed until the moon's replaced.

I listen to the frogs,
doze between ghostly bird cries.

It's past planting season,
and my soil's no longer fertile.

Contemplating Convergence

In Adoration of Savannah's Own—O'Connor, Aiken and Mercer

1.
Blue green television eyes
                              blink.
My voiceless mouth
agape
at my journal's blank page.

The news and sun
rise among banana
palms in my mind.

A train rambles by,
whistling of a time
when your Dad and I
          intertwined.

Our pink cottage,
once full of Cajun spice
and salty dreams.

Now we two remain
strangers with large pieces
of antique furniture,
obsolete as a newspapers.

Air folds heavy beside
your empty breakfast plate.

Parental planets, we circle around,
identical, irascibly sulking, until
exploding into a roar of sunlight

woven through a naked tree trunk.

My vision, delayed recognition
packed into a black business suit
while whistling for Yeats:

We've got to think free.

2.
Artists pray by creating sounds.
Mine's a Southern clang
summoned by cast iron pans.

I stiffen, mind akin to my own Daddy
who never met Mama's expectations.

He made no plans, wrinkled his
nose, secretly learned what he
wished, paging through   encyclopedias.

The ugliness of what I did and do
as scientist, architect, engineer—

I hear middle school nuns telling me:

Satan has you in his power.

A revelation:
I'm a wanton, trashy woman,
a dried up apricot named Eve
clutching onto utopian hope.

Will they carry me off in an ambulance
as the Spring sun slices whiter and hotter?

Too dehydrated for sympathetic mirrors,

I equate myself to Savannah's Sunday Brunch—

Shrimp swimming in heavy cream,
fried up, or lathered down in lard.

Elementally vulnerable, I'm perched
on a balcony sipping champagne.

The train chugs past, disappears.

3.
In my coffee mug I see a shadow
of a mountain surrounded by

clouds.

An eternal asker of answers,
I stand in the street and stare
at the stark, sunless sky.

A bell breaks memories:

The wind shrieks.
The wind grieves.

A hammer's steady crescendo
sounds the final death knell.

Released of parenting weight,
freed atoms of flesh and brain.

Pilings driven through mud,
a Fort Pulaski timber subfloor.

Somehow sunlight survives
through mold and dank dust.

Walls and roofs can be rebuilt,
a scarlet tower, made full proof.

Listen to the voices
singing far off as you
sit on the dark shore.

Keep believing
in golden scaled dragons,
griffins with rainbow wings—

Wings like swords,
an evolution of hot
and scalding white.

Write your lines,
tones falling with cold rain
like Johnny Mercer's ghost refrain:

Gather 'round, from Florida
to the North Pole holding.

When the wind is free,
when you seek sympathy,
wait for that barrel
of dynamite to detonate.

Someday church bells
will ring-a-ling for you.

Painted kites will breathe
beneath a blue umbrella sky.

4.
The first poem I shared

you caught on camera.

Infinite black and white
with mangrove honey
infused photography.

A garden of piled sand
surrounded the Sanibel
lighthouse.

Devoted to words, I wanted
to create a Cheshire Cat—

Your 5-year-old eye caught
colorful teeth and claws.

Aiken, like you, didn't consider
himself a typical southern scrawler:

 *I just wanted to master the form –
a different form every day of the year.*

Like you and me, he examined analogies
between cities and the human body—

I focus on the heart, you're
more mindful, philosophical.

Yet, we both lay word ribbons,
flat along a cracked sidewalk.

5.
In her prayer journal from 1946-47,
Flannery was just shy of 21, like you.

Like me, she started

studying journalism.

She, like you,
wished for revolution.

Fearful of mind mediocrity,
scared she'd fall prey to
intellectual quackery.

The taste of storytelling,
scotch oatmeal cookies
on her South Georgia tongue.

For you, the flavor's darker,
chocolate with a dash of sea salt.
Broken pieces made whole.

Scrapping stories Kafka-like—

Never finishing, never eating,
never completely digesting.

Both of us awaiting divinity
in a world of trumped triviality.

December Snapshot

For photographer Sally Mann and my son Sam

Be yourself; everyone else is already taken—Oscar Wilde

It's not the snaggletooth-smile,
or the perfectly pressed white dress
nor the naked nine-year-old ready
to dive into an aquatic abyss.

It's not the gnarled hands of ancient
woman juxtaposed to pudgy palms
pictured with namesake grandchild.

Not even the emaciated ribcage
of a weakening, ill suffering husband
stimulates my chilled insides.

I peek-a-boo behind my fingers
as my now grown son used to do.

Images dissolve over two decades,
Electric red to stark black-and-white.
When life squeaked fresh rather than
raised monuments to parenting death.

In the end, I am standing alone at the Getty,
at the intersection of *A Thousand Crossings*.
Iced in mommy memories until my kid cracks
a grin and declares we're both poets praying
to the elusive *angel of uncertainty*.

I thaw in response.

About the Author

Jennifer Grant is a former news journalist who resides in Gainesville, FL where she writes, edits, practices (and periodically teaches) yoga. Her first collection of poetry, *Good Form*, was published by Negative Capability Press (2017) and a chapbook, *Bronte Sisters and Beyond*, through Zoetic Press (2018). She's been nominated for a Best of 'Net and Pushcart awards. You can find more at: jenniferlynngrant.com.

God of Sparrows

by

Christina Lovin

Table of Contents

Acknowledgments

These poems have appeared in some form in the following:

Anthology of Appalachian Writers & *Escape into Life* : Fledge
Best Poem & *The Liberal Media Made Me Do It:* Writing Blindly
Ebola (anthology): What Doesn't Kill You
Gemini: 11/11/11
Hot Metal Press : As Much a Part of Earth (as "East Blue")
Naugatuck River Review : Tumor: The First Day: Double Vision
Public Republic : Ice Storm
Poemeleon: The Invisible Present
Poems of Birth : I Hold a Small Death
Schlock Magazine : Overboard
Silver Birch Press : Grave (from *All About My Name*) *Stimulus*
Respond (Britain) & *Escape into Life* : Five Hawk Day
Stimulus Respond (Britain): Why I Don't Eat Beef
under/current (Britain): A Piece of Troubled Sky
WORDPEACE : Give Me No God
Young Ravens Review : Of Rock and Ruin

Ice Storm

The snow came first, and then the rain—
it froze to everything
exposed, increased upon itself like grief
or love left unexpressed,
until the heavy branches sagged
with melancholy weight.
Some crashed to earth.
Some fingered eaves and cars.
Electric lines drew gentle arcs
of flight across the frozen air.

After all that's broken breaks,
when men with saw and axe prevail
upon the shattered places,
the sun comes back
like robins to the north in spring—
a flicker here, then full-on flocks of light
that land in trees and fields.

But at the outskirts of the town
a lumbering line: somber trucks
sag beneath their solemn loads
and wait in lines ten deep or more
to haul the ruined forests in
to where the constant plumes of smoke
ascend like ghosts of birds
on wings of ash that rise above the hills.

Five Hawk Day

On gray days such as these
a veil of frozen mist covers this flat land
where white pervades the air like dreams
of lost sailors—their empty sails,
ships passing in a fog—
small towns appear then are gone
like so many vanished hopes.

Bright days, a dozen or more
feathered shamans—signs
or fences grasped like opportunities
about to slip away. When only those
bent on good or bad are about,
just two or three raptors watch
this stretch of frozen road. They come
and wait beside the rimed roadways,
perched on wire and fence like wisdom
in a land of wandering fools,
talons of ice gripping frigid metal
with some cold patience
my frantic hours could use.

But today it is a five-hawk day:
two red tails a mile apart,
a kestrel hovering above an icy ditch.
(The one I do not count—dead
beside the road, poor wing
rising from the shoulder
as each car passes).
A pair of osprey near the river—
they disappear into the clouds above,
then plunge, indifferent,
into the bitter water below.

The Invisible Present

*Destruction is more likely to occur...
in the secrecy of the invisible present*
--John J. Magnuson

We arrive only to begin leaving, our oaths
to this earth slide into the past like light
from long-dead stars even as they are spoken
into being. We cannot comprehend
this current moment, for once we see
that it has come to be, the moment's gone
and we are rushed into the future.

So let this young Douglas fir stand here
for hope. Let its three-foot stump, forty years
hence, represent greed; the bark and shattered
limbs scattered around the clear-cut site
remind those to come that wastefulness is sin.

This battered old snag, low to the ground
but still honest in its lovely decay, can stand
for the righteousness of men; for all men,
no matter their hollowed souls, remain
upright in their own vacant eyes.

Consider the roads through the forest
as necessity: the damage they create—
nagging doubt; the child dead from
the slide of rock and mud can embody
good intentions—undeniable, immeasurable.

Felled logs along the forest floor will be
our recompense and resurrection: they flourish
even in their deaths. Mosses and lichen

are small cities of industry, forging chains
to haul the green world back from the brink.

Let this current hour show itself before
its fleeting fire goes out. Let the future
hold what we had hoped for the present,
the past again be filled with forests.
Let the invisible present be illuminated
by the strong light of truth held up
by those who stand in answer to the only
question of the spotted owl: *Who? Who?*

As Much a Part of Earth

I am afraid, I admit. There are reports of mountain lions
in these woods. I am mortal, like the deer and the squirrel,
but I come prepared: large stick in my hand, a knife
from the kitchen in my pocket. A quick study, I stop
and turn as I have read, to act as prey would: wary
and watchful. But this quiet dell is softly green
as any open meadow: a blanket of moss covering
everything, living and lost. Soon I am at peace here

like the sodden forms reclining in this gloomy glade.
Around me the apparatus of measurement (researcher's
trash, I'm told) is evident on the veiled mounds
of sawn logs: white pipes, blue flags, screens, and gauges.
Recent scrapings show bare tree flesh where scientists
have peeled off layers of the dead bark to calculate,
investigate, and adjudicate the aggregate decay. How long
does it take five-hundred-year-old wood to return to dirt?

And what is it about this place of natural decomposition
that brings to mind what lies beneath the ground?
My mother dead nearly two years now. Her mother
more than fifty, grandfather ninety years gone this spring:
should I not take comfort in their usefulness since death?
We like to measure life in years like growth rings
on a tree: my daughters, thirty-six and thirty-eight,
grown and married, their children eleven, eight,

and two, soon. (Where has the time gone? Why am I old?)
Is the lasting value of one's life actually death: how
we return to soil, even housed and sealed? We *do* return,
certain as the sun rises and sets. Dust to dust, just
as these geriatric giants do. Slowly, slowly. *Listen.*
The forest's music is sweet—a balance of life and afterlife—

77

the slow insinuation of moisture and sigh of nitrogen,
the jaws of the beetle working, their frass dropping to the sod.

Listen. Your body is already falling away. As you arrive,
you are beginning to leave, cell by cell. Be joyful, then,
my friend. For at your end your body's final uses
are no more no less than those of these boles reclining
supine and prone across the forest floor: food, shelter,
fertilizer, and nurturing soil. For all I've been in life,
to all to whom I've been anything, I say: I will turn
my back to the forest without dread. Let the lion come.
May the deer and vole and squirrel find safety today—
I sheath the jagged fear. I lay my walking stick aside
to decompose. If you believe in resurrection, believe
in this salient truth, as well: our bodies have uses
to this earth more than to any heaven you can imagine,
none more lovely than the many rooms of this jade mansion.
If I never rise better to remember me here: earthbound
in my demise, a soft mound blanketed beneath
a shroud of moss, as much a part of earth.

A Piece of Troubled Sky

I went back that way again today
where yesterday I wheeled this twisted road
just as a swallow—jubilant in its flight,
in its pursuit of bugs for summer young—
flew diversionary arcs around a truck
then struck the window of my car.

I caught a glimpse of feathered breast
like fog-veiled sun on morning fields:
a shade so pale it downed to whitest gray.
The back and wings were cruel blue—
a piece of troubled sky that fell
like hail from storm-blacked clouds.

Today I searched the road once more
where I'd watched the fallen land.
Nothing there to see—no feathers dark
as instant death and radiant as wishes.

Fledge

London, KY. (AP) - Police say a baby has died in eastern
Kentucky after a 9-year-old tripped and dropped the infant.

Because there are no proportions to death.
— Kenneth Patchen, "The Fox"

All day long I've watched them, precarious
at the edge of the windowsill: the mother
and her squabs—the nest a flat pad of grasses
on a four-inch ledge littered with the excrement
of three birds over two weeks. The fledglings'
beaks are as long as their mother's now,
but their skulls, covered with down, seem small
in comparison, dark against her mourning
gray. They stretch their wings, delicate
as a newborn's shoulder blades, lately feathered
and untried. She coddles them as they pick at her
breast, then nod in sleep, their little heads
bobbing like drowsing children.

                   A black death
descends with claw and beak—a caw!—a crow
dives toward the nest. Then the falling away
of one baby, that frantic scrabbling at the air
and the disappearing out of sight. Not yet
strong enough to fly: the breathless tumbling
through space as the watchful god of sparrows
and numbered hairs turns away. For one moment,
every bird must be there—hanging on a breath,
then gaining potential and height. But hope
is a feathered thing that drops into the pit
of my stomach, for I find nothing on the ground
below, too many long, sad stories down.

I Hold a Small Death

I hold a small death in my hands: blue
and pale, shape of a weeks-old
infant, stiff without cry or suck.

Lift it by the heels.

My body opened again: blood pulsed
between us then; now breath,
our lengthened cord.

Daughter I've borne twice: offspring
of my belly, live birth of my lungs.

Of Rock and Ruin

When you're on one, these logging roads seem small:
narrow lanes, cleared of all but gravel, grit,
and usefulness. Number 1508 winds and climbs
from Lookout Creek toward Blue River Ridge,
innocuous as the green garter snake
that crosses this bare space between the forests
with sibilant grace before my truck.

To my right, vistas sink down through trees
old as this country, then span out toward Lookout
Mountain to the East. I shift down, drive up
another rise, pull sharply left, then ease
to the right, climbing even when it seems I'm not.

The scars of logging jar my sight: a rough slough
of bared earth scours the mountainside
where the fragile road clings like desperation
or hope to the bony ledge. Dashed
against the mountain's crest, heavy clouds
split, their loads spilt with no amends
to tree or truck: water seeking its level,
roiling along the road in torrents, roaring over ridges
in brown rivers of rock and ruin.

It's hard to tell now, if the road inclines or drops
slowly down, my sense of equilibrium in this world
of two-hundred foot trunks is skewed--
the only clue the slow lowering of perspective:
trees crouching closer to the hillside
as I round a slow curve banking upward,
then stop short where a ten-foot pine stands
upright in the center of the road where rocks
and soil spill fifteen feet onto the roadway.

The hill's slide embraces the doomed tree
as I once did my dying child: knowing the truth
of life's fragility, not willing to give her up
to death. She lived. The tree will not. But
for now, ragged roots cling to this mound
of detritus torn from the clear-cut mountain's
flank. I understand that fight to stand
upright when everything around is sharp
angles and precipices, when the only level
space is narrow and hard and full of driving rain
that sluices earth from underneath
your footing, and all that remain are jagged
stone and bare roots, greedy for life.

I turn the truck around, pulling forward, rocking back,
daring myself to look over the precipice at the edge
of the road where the secret names of all things
below are *slide* or *loosen* or *release*, where old
snags hunch close to the ground beneath
the umbrella of timorous fir, and bitter
rainwater whispers the only song it's ever known
to the earth and to the listening stones.

11/11/11

In my office at the university, another day
of grading student papers and catching up
with emails, when I hear the dreadful beat
of a funeral drum: three thunderous raps
like the last heartbeats of some dying giant.
From somewhere, the sound of taps

begins playing and I remember the last time
I heard it—that bright, cold day
in April, in Illinois, as we lay Philip
next to Robert, two plots down from Kent,
each gravestone bearing the name
of a different war. I remember what day it is.

I remember my brothers, the three of them
lying close now in cold sleep as they did
as children on winter nights in a chill house,
back when their address was the same.
As it is now: Second Avenue, Knoxville
Cemetery, as if the dead need an FPO.

Outside my office window I see the flag
and below, the crowd, many dressed in black.
Their heads are bowed. I press my face
against the glass and weep. Sobbing,
the bagpipe begins to play Amazing Grace,
emptying itself again and again and again.

Tumor: The First Day: Double Vision

The mangled blue spruce next to my porch is all I see.
Or rather I see two of it, as if that symbol of my life—
stripped and mutilated—has doubled in power now.
I try not to cry, holding back the fear and tears together
as the import of what I've been told sinks in and I sit alone
in the car, one window half down, the other half up.

There used to be doves nesting in this tree each spring:
the branches so thick I couldn't see the nest
but knew it was there from the comings and goings
of the parents, the white droppings that appeared
against the cement under the huge maple shading the walk,
where the fledgling doves would wait until they could fly.

There were always two squabs, lying close along the branch
that spanned the sidewalk, then later as they grew bolder,
perpendicular. Soon they were gone. Now the doubled
branches that remain on the spruce are sparse
as my eyebrows. I can draw those in, darken the skin
so that it appears I am normal. The tree is out of luck.

There is no dark mass pressing on its nerves, doubling
everything viewed, creating a world of mirrors: double cars,
twin lights, people like Siamese twins walking closely—
arm in arm and leg in leg—along the street by my house.
There will be no more doves knitting together a home
among those branches: no twosomes, no couples, no pairs.

The tree is doomed: spruces can't grow their branches back.
Spindly fronds shoot out between the stumps of missing limbs
along the barren trunk, no chance of being more than twigs.
The tree should be cut down, sawn and hauled away,
but it is over sixty years old. I can't bear to simply kill it.
My own luck lies in tests to come, the surgeon's many knives.

Grave

Christina Ericson
1875-1906

Christina was her name, as well as mine.
We never met, but yet, I carry her
Nordic blood, her dark hair and hazel eyes.

She gave her life giving my father his—
1906, midwife with dirty hands—
seven days in August and she was gone.

Did she ever hold his tiny body
to her poisonous breast? Her own body
a gate slammed shut, become a rankling wound.

That loss defined him for nearly ninety years:
rootless soul still yearning for that family tree,
one branch severed at the decaying trunk—

a pain passed down in DNA we're told
today—now mine as I regard her grave.
My name incised in stone there, first and last.

What Doesn't Kill You

Louisville, Ky. — A Kentucky company used local
tobacco to help produce an experimental serum to fight Ebola

Drive down any road here and you'll see it:
row upon row of green—pale in the spring
then darker as the seasons make their change

through summer's heat and storm, into the fall
when what was vibrant fades to golden hues.
Then stripped, staked, and crucified in the fields.

Slouching to leather, tanned soft as the skin
of chamois, hung to dry in the rafters
of black barns, their doors open like the mouths

of the cancerous dead and dying. Now
a world away another death: *Ebola.*
What doesn't kill you and all that, right?

The key to saving lives seems now to lie
in the contagion that destroys five million
others every year. It's that time again:

here strips of brown tobacco leaves blow loose
along the narrow country roads. They writhe
and slither like Eden's serpent, whispering:

You will certainly not die.

Unseasonable

December 14, 2012

After the meteor shower
after the shower of bullets
after the bodies and the blood
outside in unseasonable air
outside a summer fog rises in December
outside the peepers are singing
as if no child were lying dead
as if the world could continue
as if it can or will.

Why I Don't Eat Beef

Like young dogs the calves chase each other
then gather to lie down next to a stream,
their knobby knees scuffed and stained
with pasture grasses. Heads too big
for their bodies, nodding until they give in
to sleep. They are tired from their youthfulness
just as their mothers, like any mothers,
are wearied from their duties of motherhood—
the watchfulness, the worry.

On hot days they slide down into farm ponds,
stand withers deep to cool themselves. I imagine
them exchanging pleasantries or gossip
like teenage girls at the lake or pool.

If I stop beside their field, they come, curious as cats
to see who it is that visits. When I stand near the fence
they draw nearer to me, my humanness mirrored
in the depths of those eyes that appear
somewhat like souls: some other creature
who like them is gentle and slow.

Sometimes I see them yearning their gazes
across a country road where grass is always greener,
and know their intent, their longing, their fear
that something is being missed,
that something better must lie over that hill.

Then when the field yawns open and emptied,
their absence is like a bolt shot through my mind.
For like the young soldiers I have witnessed
moving like steers through the terminal—
unaware of what lies ahead—they did not know

they were nothing but meat
to be ground for some ravenous red hunger.

Give Me No God

Give me no god
that will kill
children indiscriminately
sever the limbs
of women or men
or crush the skulls
or spirits of anyone
for land or minerals
or petroleum
bought at a price
of bloody ditches
full of the dead and dying
along the highways
where tanker trucks
and pilgrims travel
side-by-side
with armies of the right
or wrong—that god
does not exist
there is no god
like that but if
there should be
give me no god
at all.

Overboard

All seas, all straits, all bays, all gulfs—
I'd like to clutch them to my breast,
feel them in my arms and die!
-Fernando Pessoa as Álvero de Campos

Some things, they are a mercy not to know—
like how to swim when trawling out on open sea.
Old fishermen know it is better not to fight
when fallen overboard into the frigid sluice.
Three minutes if you're lucky. Five or six
if you try to save yourself. *Fool.* Struggling
just prolongs the pain. While those at rail
and wheel who watch in vain can only cross
themselves above the churning foam. So close
your arms around your chest. Let out
your breath and simply slide beneath the wake.
There is no point in lowering the boats.

Writing Blindly

I am writing blindly.
      —Dimitri Kolexnikov, of the doomed Russian
        submarine, Kursk, in a letter to his wife

This is my dying
message. I am dying.
My message may live. I would
write in blood without
an instrument, with my finger-
nails, with intense pain on the stone
wall of my prison, the rusted
door of this crypt, inside
the coffin lid—scratches, clawings.
Symbols that are untranslatable
to calm eyes, unutterable
to steady voices.

I want to tell you to sing
because a song is sweeter
in the dark, to tell you the dark
is sweeter than light, that light
is sweeter than death, that death
is light when inhalation becomes
the rumor of a dead man's
smile, and pulse
is a lie of rhythm;
when all that can be
written is the myth.

I am writing blindly
	in the language of the living
		who are already dead.

I am writing blindly.

	Like all of us.

About the author

Christina Lovin is a native Mid-Westerner born in Galesburg, Illinois, the hometown of fellow Swedish poet Carl Sandburg. She now makes her home in Central Kentucky, where she lives with a varying number of rescue dogs in a town reminiscent of Mayberry. After having several careers, including minister's wife, retail shop owner, and VISTA volunteer, she received a Master of Fine Arts in Creative Writing from New England College. Lovin is currently a Senior Lecturer in the English Department at Eastern Kentucky University and contributing faculty to the EKU MFA program: Bluegrass Writers Studio. Lovin's writing has appeared in over one hundred different literary journals (most recently, *New Millennium, Hayden's Ferry Review,* and *Contrapasso*) and anthologies (*Universal Oneness: An Anthology of Magnum Opus Poems From Around the World, The Doll Collection,* and *Intimacy: An Anthology*), as well as five volumes of poetry (*Echo, A Stirring in the Dark, Flesh, Little Fires,* and *What We Burned for Warmth*). She is the recipient of numerous poetry awards, writing residencies, fellowships, and grants, most notably the AWP Kurt Brown Scholarship, the Stone Coast Baron Wormser Scholarship, Antioch Writers' Conference Judson Jerome Scholarship, the Al Smith Fellowship from Kentucky Arts Council, several grants from the Kentucky Foundation for Women, and an Elizabeth George Foundation Grant.

Critical Praise

Edgar Degas once said, "Art is not what you see but what you make others see." In *Self-Portraits*, Lang spotlights the work of twenty-three women artists. Here, poets, designers, and more revel in "this power to make new things" from war, grief, poverty, dailiness, alienation. "Constant and unforgiving, Unwilling to turn away," Lang's is a piercing light. She "does the work of earthworms, breaks the image down, so you see the form that burns." These viscerally moving poems will sear your memory. "The room hums with their voices / like a church where the organ has just finished playing." Bask in this music and be born. —Angela Narciso Torres, *Author of Blood Orange, To the Bone,* and *What Happens is Neither*

To read Susanna Lang's poems in *Self-Portraits* is to get a glimpse into the imagined lives of her subjects and, at the same time, share in her own reflections on what it means to be an artist. Reaching out across artistic forms and passing through time, *Self-Portraits* is Lang's conversation with fellow artists—all women who have immersed themselves in this lifeline to being. Each has a rich lived experience that intertwines in Ms. Lang's poetry. Here is Alice Neel, sitting in her studio, aged, ready to paint...

> *"She has a brush in one hand, paint rag in the other.*
> *Nothing else, not even clothes.*
>
> *Yes, her breasts sag.*
> *Her belly sits in her lap like a child.*
>
> *But look at her right foot-*
> *Flexed, ready to go..."*

There is Artremesia Gentilleschi, a great painter alone in a world dominated by men, confident and somehow whole. Kathe Kollwitz, persevering through years of loss and grief yet always strong in her compassion. In this thoughtful and richly rewarding new book of poetry, Lang takes us on a new journey with these artists. Aligned in all is a sense of mystery alongside vivid specificity. There is a sense of highly personal translation that we become a part of through her poetry and that replenishes us. —*Alan Loehle is a painter and a Professor of Studio Art at Oglethorpe University.*

"One of the most striking aspects of Jennifer Grant's talent is her poetic ear. Each line in her poems bear her unmistakable, singular poetic voice that takes measure of the human heart as it reveals an abiding reverence for and love of family and place. The eloquence of her poetic lines present a treasure trove of poems such as the unforgettable ""Mid May just Before the Flower Moon Blooms," "Contemplating Convergence During A Savannah Sojourn To Visit My Soon-to-Graduate Son," and "December Snapshot." Grant knows how to shape memory into a masterpiece of craft." —Sue Walker, publisher of Negative Capability Press, Professor Emerita at the University of South Alabama and a former Poet Laureate of Alabama.

Christina Lovin's chapbook *God of Sparrows* contains a good many birds (five crows, two squabs and multiple fledglings), a tribute to majestic trees, and poems about both large and small deaths, including a poem about the tragic loss of her three brothers to three different wars. The poem from which the title comes, "Fledge," is a powerful, moving narrative poem, beautifully crafted: *She coddles them as they pick at her/breast, then nod in sleep, their little heads/bobbing like drowsing children. // A black death/descends with claw and beak—a caw! —a crow/dives toward the nest. Then the falling away/ of one baby, that frantic scrabbling at the air/and the disappearing out of sight...*Lovin's images in this poem serve to entice the reader into a sense of comfort, then a sudden turn, punctuated in a concrete way by the right-alignment of the words "a

98

black death" and em dashes, as the heart-stopping calls of the mother bird and the crow intersect in that next line. We see the nestling fall and feel the impetus to fly and catch it as our breath is stolen by this poem. *God of Sparrows* is not a tame book. It is a wild journey, which the reader will find both powerfully moving and uplifting. —Lori Desrosiers, author of *Keeping Planes in the Air* (Salmon Poetry)

Christina Lovin's wry, elegant, heartfelt elegies in *God of Sparrows* honor our resilience in the face of peril—losses private and global, pains intimately felt and shared, crises of faith and crises of environment. Mostly, her keen eye turns to the natural world, to landscapes that are expressionistic of our inner lives. In encounters with disasters and illness, hunger and heartbreak, Lovin's poems are attuned to vulnerability—"I am afraid, I admit," she writes, in one poem—as well as to the subtle changes that forebode even darker realities—"There used to be doves nesting in this tree each spring." But even in these lyrical explorations of death, Lovin can feel the rhythms of a living nature, terrifying and beautiful, its primal push and pull. —Richie Hofmann, *Second Empire*

-
-
-
-
-

More from BLP

Delphi Series Vol. 1

Anna Leahy
Karen L. George
Robert Perry Ivey

Delphi Series Vol. 2

Joy Ladin
Jennifer Litt
Tasha Cotter

Delphi Series Vol. 3

Aaron Bauer
Francine Rubin
Meghan Sterling

Delphi Series Vol. 4

Ting Gou
Claire Zoghb
Erin Redfern

Delphi Series Vol. 5 (fiction)

Diane Payne
Lana Spendl
Chella Courington

Delphi Series Vol. 6

Allison Blevins
Saul Hillel Benjamin
Cameron Morse

Delphi Series Vol. 7

Marjorie Power
Sally Zakariya
Martha McCollough

Delphi Series Vol. 8

Charlette Mandel
Carly Sachs
Lois Marie Harrod

Delphi Series Vol. 9 (this issue)

Susanna Lang
Jennifer Grant
Christina Lovin

www.ingramcontent.com/pod-product-compliance
Lightning Source LLC
LaVergne TN
LVHW041302080426
835510LV00009B/842